BLACK VOICES ON RACE

SIDNEY POITIER

by Anitra E. Butler-Ngugi

FOCUS
READERS.
NAVIGATOR

WWW.FOCUSREADERS.COM

Focus Readers is distributed by North Star Editions:
sales@northstareditions.com | 888-417-0195

Produced for Focus Readers by Red Line Editorial.

Content Consultant: Keith M. Harris, PhD, Associate Professor of Media & Cultural Studies, University of California, Riverside

Photographs ©: World History Archive/Alamy, cover, 1; Anitra Butler-Ngugi, 2; Columbia Pictures/Photofest, 4–5, 18–19; AP Images, 7, 23; Keystone View Company/Library of Congress, 8–9; Shutterstock Images, 11, 12–13, 17, 25; Angelo Rizzuto/Anthony Angel Collection/Library of Congress, 15; CX/AP Images, 21; J. Scott Applewhite/AP Images, 26–27; Red Line Editorial, 29

Library of Congress Cataloging-in-Publication Data
Names: Butler-Ngugi, Anitra E., author.
Title: Sidney Poitier / by Anitra E. Butler-Ngugi.
Description: Lake Elmo, MN : Focus Readers, [2023] | Series: Black voices on race | Includes index. | Audience: Grades: 4–6
Identifiers: LCCN 2022005195 (print) | LCCN 2022005196 (ebook) | ISBN 9781637392683 (hardcover) | ISBN 9781637393208 (paperback) | ISBN 9781637394205 (pdf) | ISBN 9781637393727 (ebook)
Subjects: LCSH: Poitier, Sidney--Juvenile literature. | Poitier, Sidney--Influence--Juvenile literature. | African American motion picture actors and actresses--Biography. | Race in motion pictures. | Motion pictures--United States--History--20th century. | United States--Race relations--History--20th century.
Classification: LCC PN2287.P57 B88 2023 (print) | LCC PN2287.P57 (ebook) | DDC 791.4302/8092 [B]--dc23/eng/20220331
LC record available at https://lccn.loc.gov/2022005195
LC ebook record available at https://lccn.loc.gov/2022005196

Printed in the United States of America
Mankato, MN
082022

ABOUT THE AUTHOR

Anitra E. Butler-Ngugi is a reading teacher, writer, college professor, and author of children's books. She loves to travel and make YouTube videos. She lives in Maryland with her husband.

TABLE OF CONTENTS

CHAPTER 1

RACE ON THE BIG SCREEN

Loving someone your family objects to can be hard. The movie *Guess Who's Coming to Dinner* explores this idea. In the movie, a Black man and a white woman are in love. The movie came out in 1967. In the 1960s, many people disapproved of **interracial** relationships. In fact, these relationships were illegal

Guess Who's Coming to Dinner was the first Hollywood movie to give an interracial relationship a happy ending.

in many American states. But the movie showed the relationship in a positive way.

Sidney Poitier played the main male character, Dr. John Prentice. In one explosive scene, Dr. Prentice scolds his father. He says, "You think of yourself as a colored man. I think of myself as a man."[1] In other words, the father defines himself by his race. He lives in a society in which race matters. Dr. Prentice, however, defines himself as an individual. He lives in a society in which race *shouldn't* matter.

This scene touched many in the audience. It was one of several scenes in which Poitier's character commented

1. *Guess Who's Coming to Dinner*. Directed by Stanley Kramer, Columbia Pictures. 1967.

In 1967, the US Supreme Court ended bans on interracial marriage. Mildred and Richard Loving challenged the law.

on society. Poitier used his acting talent to explore race, prejudice, and more. He chose roles that expanded how white society viewed Black Americans.

CHAPTER 2

BORN TO WALK WITH KINGS

Sidney Poitier was born on February 20, 1927, in Miami, Florida. His parents were tomato farmers from The Bahamas. They brought Sidney back to The Bahamas. They raised him on Cat Island.

Sidney worked on the farm along with his siblings. He also acted for fun. Sidney made costumes out of old clothes.

Sidney Poitier had dual citizenship in both the United States and The Bahamas.

He created characters. Then he wrote scenes for them. Sidney's sister once asked him what he wanted to do with his life. At age 12, he already knew. He wanted to be an actor.

Race did not matter much to Sidney growing up. On Cat Island, there was no

FATED FOR FAME

Sidney was born two months early. His father thought he wouldn't survive. But Sidney's mother didn't want to give up. She asked a soothsayer for advice. A soothsayer is a person who claims to see the future. This person told her that Sidney would be fine. In fact, he would become rich and famous. He would carry the Poitier name all over the world.

Cat Island is a quiet and rural part of The Bahamas. It has no major cities and a small population.

need to see himself as a person of color. Almost everyone on the island looked like him. Then Sidney moved to Miami to live with his brother. He was not prepared for the racism he would experience there.

CHAPTER 3

MAKING HIS OWN OPPORTUNITY

Sidney Poitier faced discrimination and danger in Miami. He even had a scary encounter with the **Ku Klux Klan**. At age 16, he'd had enough. Sidney left Miami for New York City.

Opportunities were hard to find. Sidney worked as a dishwasher. He slept on the streets until he could afford to rent

Harlem is a neighborhood in New York City. It was the center of a Black cultural movement in the 1920s and 1930s.

a room. But he still didn't earn enough money for warm clothing. To avoid New York's cold winter, he joined the US Army. After a year in the army, he returned to New York to try again.

RULES AROUND RACE

In Miami in the early 1940s, there were many rules around race. For example, Black people were allowed to use only the back doors at white homes and businesses. Sidney didn't know these rules. He delivered a package to a woman's front door. Angered, members of the Ku Klux Klan searched for Sidney at his brother's house. Fortunately, Sidney wasn't home. But the event scared him. He moved to another neighborhood. Later, he moved from Miami altogether.

Times Square is a famous area in New York City. Even in the 1940s, it was a hub for entertainment.

Poitier came across the American Negro Theatre. At the time, it was the most famous Black theater in the United States. Poitier tried out for a role. The director rejected him because of his accent and his limited reading skills.

Poitier saw this as a challenge. He continued working as a dishwasher. But he also spent months improving his reading skills. He changed his accent by listening to the radio. He also volunteered as a janitor in the theater in exchange for acting classes.

Poitier soon got an opportunity to show his skills. He performed in the lead role of a student production. A **Broadway** director saw his acting. The director gave Poitier a part in *Lysistrata*, an ancient Greek play. Poitier made his Broadway debut in 1946. He got his lines wrong

Broadway is a long street in New York City. Dozens of professional theaters are located along the street.

in the first performance. But audiences enjoyed his acting. And Poitier was determined to be successful. Soon, new opportunities came Poitier's way.

CHAPTER 4

CHALLENGING HOLLYWOOD

There wasn't much work for Black actors on Broadway in the late 1940s. So, Sidney Poitier moved to California. His first film role was in the 1950 movie *No Way Out*. The movie was one of the first to directly address racism. Poitier played a Black doctor under attack by a racist white man.

Sidney Poitier performed in *A Raisin in the Sun*. This play is about the everyday life and struggles of a working-class Black family.

At the time, Black actors were mostly stuck playing servants or other small roles. Many of these roles showed Black people in a negative way. But Poitier played an intelligent, **dignified** doctor. His powerful acting helped audiences see Black people in a new way. In fact, Poitier refused roles that showed Black people as powerless. He also refused roles that contributed to racial **stereotypes**.

Poitier acted in several movies in the 1950s. He also continued to perform on Broadway. Many of his films and plays explored racism. For example, *The Defiant Ones* was released in 1958. Poitier played a prisoner who works with

At the 1958 Berlin Film Festival, Poitier won an award for his performance in *The Defiant Ones*.

a white prisoner to escape. The two must put aside their prejudices to avoid getting caught. The movie called for people of different races to work together. Poitier was nominated for the Academy Award for Best Actor for his role.

Poitier rose to fame as the first Black movie star. In 1964, he broke another barrier. Poitier won the Academy Award for Best Actor for his role in *Lilies of the Field*. He was the first Black person to win this award.

Despite his success, Poitier also received criticism. The 1960s saw the rise of the **Black Power** movement. The decade also saw the **assassinations** of Martin Luther King Jr. and Malcolm X. These men were key figures in the civil rights movement. It was a time of great change for the Black community. Some Black people criticized Poitier for not doing enough. They felt he chose roles that were not threatening to white people. They wanted him to be a **revolutionary**.

Poitier was arguably the world's most famous actor in 1967. He starred in three of the year's biggest films.

Poitier took these criticisms to heart. He returned to The Bahamas. He took some time away from acting. He wanted to think about how he would approach race in the future.

RACIAL EQUALITY

Cry, the Beloved Country came out in 1951. The movie is about apartheid. Apartheid was a system of racial segregation in South Africa. It lasted from the late 1940s until the 1990s.

Sidney Poitier traveled to South Africa to make the film. He experienced the cruelty of apartheid while filming. For example, there were separate bathrooms for Black people and white people. The bathroom for Black people was dirty. So, Poitier used the "whites only" bathroom. Later, white people with guns chased him to the airport.

In 1997, Poitier returned to South Africa for another movie. By this time, apartheid had ended. Nelson Mandela was serving as the country's first Black president. Before becoming president, Mandela had been an anti-apartheid activist.

Nelson Mandela was sworn in as the president of South Africa in 1994.

Poitier played him in the movie *Mandela and de Klerk*.

In his roles, Poitier always sought to promote racial equality. Reporters often asked him about race and racism. But this frustrated Poitier. He did not want to be defined by his race.

CHAPTER 5

HOLLYWOOD LEGEND

In the 1970s and beyond, Sidney Poitier did more than just act. He also directed movies. Many of these films were comedies. In addition, Poitier entered international politics. He represented The Bahamas at UNESCO. This organization promotes culture, education, and scientific achievement.

Sidney Poitier receives the Presidential Medal of Freedom in 2009.

Poitier continued to act through the early 2000s. He remained focused on roles that promoted racial equality. For example, *Separate but Equal* was a television miniseries. Poitier played Thurgood Marshall. Marshall was the first Black justice on the US Supreme Court.

MAJOR AWARDS

In 2001, Sidney Poitier was awarded a second Academy Award. He earned a Special Award for Lifetime Achievement. In 2009, Poitier received the Presidential Medal of Freedom. This is the highest honor that a US civilian can earn. President Barack Obama gave Poitier the award. Obama was the country's first Black president.

Poitier died in January 2022. In his lifetime, Poitier acted in more than 50 movies and TV shows. He also directed nine movies. In the roles he chose, he changed the film industry. He expanded the opportunities for other Black actors. Many people consider Poitier a Hollywood legend.

SIDNEY POITIER TIMELINE

1927	1950	1951	1964	1967	1991	1997	2009	2022

Makes his film debut in *No Way Out*

Wins the Academy Award for Best Actor for *Lilies of the Field*

Stars in the TV miniseries *Separate but Equal*

Is awarded the Presidential Medal of Freedom by President Barack Obama

Born in Miami, Florida

Acts in *Cry, the Beloved Country*

Stars in *Guess Who's Coming to Dinner*

Stars in *Mandela and de Klerk*

Dies in January

FOCUS ON
SIDNEY POITIER

Write your answers on a separate piece of paper.

1. Write a paragraph summarizing the main ideas of Chapter 4.

2. Sidney Poitier was both praised and criticized for the roles he chose. Do you think he made a difference in the film industry and in society? Why or why not?

3. For which film did Poitier earn an Academy Award?
   A. *Guess Who's Coming to Dinner*
   B. *Lilies of the Field*
   C. *Cry, the Beloved Country*

4. How might Poitier's childhood in The Bahamas have helped him challenge American society's views of Black people?
   A. Poitier didn't speak with an American accent and didn't know how to read well.
   B. Poitier chose only roles that showed Black people in a negative way.
   C. Poitier was not raised to follow certain rules of race or think of himself as Black.

Answer key on page 32.

GLOSSARY

assassinations
The murders of famous people, often political leaders.

Black Power
A movement that began in the 1960s and focused on Black pride and self-reliance as opposed to integration with white society.

Broadway
An area in New York City where there are many theaters.

dignified
Having a serious, calm manner that commands respect.

interracial
Referring to relationships between people of different races.

Ku Klux Klan
An American terrorist hate group that has targeted Black people and other minority groups since the 1860s.

revolutionary
A person who supports extreme changes in government or society.

stereotypes
Overly simple and harmful ideas of how all members of a certain group are.

TO LEARN MORE

BOOKS

Castro, Emanuel. *Nelson Mandela*. North Mankato, MN: Capstone Press, 2018.

Fishman, Jon M. *Martin Luther King Jr.: Walking in the Light*. Minneapolis: Lerner Publications, 2019.

Green, Amanda Jackson. *Diversity and Entertainment: Black Lives in Media*. Minneapolis: Lerner Publications, 2021.

NOTE TO EDUCATORS

Visit **www.focusreaders.com** to find lesson plans, activities, links, and other resources related to this title.

INDEX

Answer Key: **1.** Answers will vary; **2.** Answers will vary; **3.** B; **4.** C